No Diplomacy

ANDREW LAFLECHE

No Diplomacy
Copyright © 2015 Andrew Lafleche
www.AJLafleche.com

Cover design by eBook Launch
Cover photo by Anja Niedringhaus

ISBN: 0-994-79010-4
ISBN-13: 978-0-994-79010-1

First Edition: April 2015

10 9 8 7 6 5 4 3 2 1

FOR ANJA

CONTENTS

"WE DON'T LIKE TO KILL OUR
UNBORN, WE NEED THEM TO
GROW UP AND FIGHT OUR WARS."

Marylin Manson, *The High End of Low*

PREFACE

Ever since I came back, you've been telling me that something is wrong. That I should talk about it. Why? So you can live vicariously through my half-truths. Even if I told you, you could never understand. That's the great problem with consciousness: how does it feel? Philosopher Thomas Nigel, in his article entitled "What is it like to be a bat?" addresses the subjective character of experience. You could know all there is to know about how a bat maneuvers its way through the night by sonar, but in the end you still don't know how it feels to be a bat. Without actually experiencing the moment, you never will. Alas, I am exhausted by everyone else's atrocious stories that I now submit my own.

The first thing you'll undoubtedly ask is if I've killed someone? What a cowardly poised question.

I should strike you. Have I killed someone?

Vicarious faggot.

Somebody once asked me why we didn't notice the bomb that blew us up and nearly ended our meagre existence.

Really? Why didn't we uncover the strategically placed IED that was specifically positioned to cause the most destruction to opposing combatants?

Fuck you.

Maybe that morning we thought it would be exciting to play a game of Russian roulette.

How was it? Really? A casual "how was it?"

Go to hell.

That's why I don't talk to herd's people.

Stupid questions invite stupid answers.

Here you go.

CHAPTER ONE

Once upon a time not long ago, I was savouring the sweet aroma of a neatly poured glass of Johnny Walker Black Label when in my stupor I conjured up the idea of going to war. How grand! I could nobly volunteer my services, receive a sizable paycheck, be trained to become effective with all sorts of weaponry and then travel abroad to go exercise these newly acquired skills on third world peasants. A quick comparison of the large number of soldiers who have deployed and returned from Afghanistan versus the significantly lower number of soldiers who have deployed and not returned led me to believe that my odds of survival were pretty good.

If you ever want to evaluate the risk of something, run the numbers. Numbers don't lie.

A couple more glasses of scotch and several invigorating combat videos later, I completed the recruiting center's online application to become an infanteer. When I did not receive an instant response to my honest efforts, I decided to continue to saturate my body with whiskey.

In the morning, I continued on my merry little way, not giving a second thought about the army. Imagine my surprise when I received a call from a Master something or a Sergeant type individual a few months later. He was inquiring whether I was still interested in enlisting with the Forces.

Sure, I thought. Why not?

We arranged a date for an interview and aptitude test, the latter which I aced or nearly so, landing myself in the ninety-seventh percentile. This allowed me the opportunity to select virtually any trade in the military. Despite being encouraged to consider one of the more glamorous positions, I decided to adhere to my initial choice of becoming an infantry soldier. I figured they could go fuck themselves; I wanted to do the shit I saw in the movies.

A little hung over and still able to taste the coke in the back of my throat from partying the night before, I didn't have the patience to dance. Infantry it was.

All this nonsense bores me, but I wanted to illustrate to you the whimsical decision it was to sign up. It's nauseating to hear about some mythical sacrifice I've made or about how noble it was for me to stand up for democracy or risk my life for this country.

Patriotism's a joke.

If you were born 'there,' or anywhere else that's away from 'here' for that matter, you'd be just as fucking patriotic.

Don't act all high and mighty because you won the ovarian lottery by being born in the country where Jesus was. You had just as much control over that, as you do over what I tell you.

Likewise, it's just as appalling for you to tell me how you

would have enlisted if it wasn't for some 'insert your cowardly excuse here.'

But I digress.

The purpose of the second meeting with 'Sarge' was to sign a large yellow contract and inform me that I would leave in a week's time in order to begin the upcoming basic training cycle.

My boss wasn't too happy that I didn't give him the heads up or adequate notice or whatever, but I didn't care; I was going to war. With any luck he'd see me on the front page of some newspaper praising my heroic efforts. Unfortunately, this didn't happen; a picture of me with a sunflower tucked into the scrim of my helmet did end up circulating online news.

I packed my bags, boarded a shitty little plane in some back country airport, and took off for thirteen weeks of washed-up soldiers trying to shove their dicks in my ass.

CHAPTER TWO

If I could go back and do basic training again I don't think I'd make it.

They'd cut me for sure.

You see, unless you're trying to get some check in the box in order to progress your career, the only soldiers who staff the basic training facilities are there to be kept away from their units. Insubordination would be my death. Basic training and battle school systematically removes the hard-core assholes, the punks who only signed up to prove something to someone elsewhere. The system is far from perfect, so undoubtedly some of those pricks make it through and continue to get promoted and posted up the ranks only to lead new troops to certain death or dismemberment. Three of which people were fired from my tour for countless indiscretions causing much harm to many of my comrades.

Or, they remain tucked away at the schools to keep them

from causing said early demise.

The army is similar to high school in some ways, a bunch of boys who never grew up. Myself included. People seeking refuge in something bigger than themselves, looking to attribute meaning to this otherwise accidental existence. It's sort of amusing to witness the inner workings of our Armed Forces.

Before I knew it, I was a full-fledged regular force soldier, lowest on the rank structure and in line for every shitty task that came up.

I began training for my tour in Afghanistan.

After not enough time at the shooting range, too many sleepless nights, and a tremendous amount of alcohol, I was ready to deploy to The Sandbox.

Sometimes we called Afghanistan, The Sandbox.

I share all of this with you as though speaking in a single breath and the time passed quickly for me, but in reality training took somewhere in the range of two tedious years to complete. If interested in that bullshit, you can tantalize your desire to 'experience' the details in the nauseating array of already published tales which line some section of your favourite book store.

CHAPTER THREE

Fast forward to the future, which is inevitably the past, and we boarded another shitty plane to fly us to a third party destination. From there we flew to a secret base 'that doesn't exist', in order to board a military flight. This last plane would insert us into Afghanistan. The vacationing soldiers at the secret base (who I refer to as 'vacationing' because they'll never see combat or risk anything except obesity and sexually transmitted diseases) stamped my passport incorrectly, causing a significant hassle returning to Canada on leave. Unfortunately, while fabricating mine, they made it appear as if I'd been in Dubai for only twenty-four hours.

Who visits Dubai for one day?

Anyways, Afghanistan is beautiful.

I mean that. The contrast of the desert sand with its foliage heightens the greens to a level I've never seen either before or since. It's vibrant; like gazing into the Secret Garden while tumbling down the Rabbit Hole.

It's also one of the many reasons why Afghanistan is the greatest place in the world. If there weren't so many assholes residing there, I'd genuinely consider paying a visit. Maybe even relocating. Why not? The pot plants are larger than Christmas trees and grow in fields three times the size of those which accommodate football. Ounces of hash are only a few bucks American, and you can buy ten dollar cell phones that come with unlimited airtime plans.

Yes sir, get rid of the bullies and watch Afghanistan become the next best vacation destination.

Kandahar Airfield. KAF. The super-base housing thousands of international soldiers, many of whom never leave their air conditioned offices or accommodations. These are the 'soldiers' who complain about the lineups at Tim Horton's and participate in ball hockey tournaments. KAF is where all the celebrities visit.

That's not entirely true.

One time we were graced by the presence of celebrities at our camp. They dismounted the helicopter and scurried into the only concrete building we had, while we all waited outside to meet them. After a short time with us roasting in the desert sun and them swapping niceties with the self-appointed elite inside, they hurried back onto the chopper which would escort them safely back to wherever they came from.

If you want to remember how to spell desert correctly, as opposed to dessert, think to yourself "which would you rather have multiples of: the scorching heat of the sun, or succulent sweets?" There's a double's' in the latter.

Oh yes, before I forget, eat shit KAFites (the people who live in KAF). You jack us up because our combats are dirty and speckled with blood. You reprimand us because our boots aren't bloused and the hair on our face is not neatly shaven.

How about you live outside the wire for six months or more and eat rations for every meal?

How about you live with the ever plaguing question of whether your next step will be your last?

Get fucked.

These are the majority of people coming back with PTSD and making a big stink that they're combat veterans. These are the majority of people who shut the fuck up in the presence of an infanteer, engineer, or any other front line soldier.

I know, I know, the people 'serving' there are just as necessary as we are. We couldn't operate without their support, because they supply our rations and gear and blah, blah, blah.

You shouldn't wear the same medal as us.

Period.

CHAPTER FOUR

Kandahar Air Field. We arrived, were briefed, and then issued our mission-specific gear. We were then bussed to a secure range so that we could test our weapons before boarding the helicopter that would relocate us to our new home for the next two hundred and some-odd days. We had a good laugh at the range because some multi-star general negligently discharged his weapon and got away with it. One of our guys did the same thing after a couple of sleepless nights on operation but was charged sixteen hundred bucks. It probably had something to do with the fact that our guy almost shot the person riding in the vehicle in front of his, but whatever. One of the benefits of being a Higher-up, I guess.

I think that this general was the same dude who was fired for fucking his clerk. It doesn't matter though; they're all the same egotistical pricks anyways. Remember that murdering, rapist Colonel from Trenton?

The next morning, while heading to the mess hall for breakfast just before mounting the helicopter which would fly us to our camp, a rocket was launched into the grid of KAF.

"Rocket Attack. Rocket Attack," boomed over the loudspeakers.

You should have seen all the people rushing for cover. Don't these pricks realize that once the alarm sounds, it's likely too late? Laughing hysterically, we snapped a selfie to document the occasion, before snagging the empty spaces in the food line-up. If we had to do a tour in KAF, we probably would have been sent home for treating the base with the contempt it deserves.

After breakfast, a bus transported us across the base to the airstrip, where we were lined up in a pretty little row. One little, two little, three little idiots, all dressed up to die.

The exhaust from the helicopter's engine singed my face as we filed into its fuselage.

I don't remember how long the flight was, but several evasive maneuvers later we began our descent into Strong Point 'can't tell you the name'.

CHAPTER FIVE

Have you ever seen the film Jarhead? Welcome to the suck.

Having been privy to a blast, I can tell you first-hand that the scene where the guy is having all those mortars pop off around him, and it's dark and hazy and he can't hear shit, is pretty bang on the actual event.

Jarhead is the only war movie I've ever enjoyed. I once tried watching Generation Kill while over there and almost lost my mind.

I guess I should set the stage for you. There was some superhero operation underway involving our small-armed officer in charge; quite literally, one of his arms was micro-sized. It was fucking freaky. Well, he had developed a plan.

Actually, first let's get back to his arm. One time I had to shake this monstrosity while receiving a promotion and my hand swallowed his like a whore's vagina would swallow a cock. It was like rolling a hotdog down the hall.

Anyways, back to the brilliant plan. He developed the bright idea to deploy all of the members of our camp except for six who were to be held back in order to maintain security. I was one of those six; I may have even been in charge. I figured, fuck it. If shit was to go down we wouldn't stand a chance, so I smoked a bowl of Afghanistan's finest and booted up my laptop to watch Generation Kill.

Worst idea ever.

Every time a bomb went off on screen, I thought one was going off in our camp. Needless to say, which is a stupid expression because it always prefaces that which is being said; I never finished watching the series.

When our chopper finally touched down, we rushed off with all of our gear and exchanged devious smiles with the soldiers who we were relieving as they filed past us. We were like virgins about to lose our innocence in the back of some beat up station wagon.

The few soldiers who remained from the exiting rotation (ROTO) gave us a detailed handover before evacuating during the ensuing week.

We'd finally arrived; our little vacation from the real world where we would no longer have to worry about paying bills or keeping up with the Jones'. We would no longer have to deal with the television telling us which pop star was headed off to rehab. The only activities to occupy our agenda would be making sure that our fire-team partners stayed alive so that they could watch our own backs, and wonder about who our wives would be fucking in our absence.

Afghanistan is notorious for breaking up relationships. It's almost worth putting money down on whose would end first.

CHAPTER SIX

Our company was divided into three locations, and I boast that our platoon received the best one. Our fierce brothers in the first platoon got the short end of the stick and were in contact daily.

Contact is conflict; a gunfight or a bomb blast.

Our other boys were fucked into living with a bunch of Sergeant Majors who were playing pissy match with their authority. This was before being sent off to a shithole, similar to the first platoon's location, for the last couple of months.

I don't understand Sergeant Majors overseas. Sergeant Majors are pretty much the highest working rank of the non-commission rank structure. These guys impose all sorts of rules upon the soldiers who serve beneath them, rules which play no role in affecting survival or the success of combat missions. Who really gives a fuck if we're shaven or our pant legs aren't bloused? If you're comfortable, you perform a hell of a lot better.

Could they be that scared of their surroundings that in order to create the facade of control they feel the need to exercise their fleeting authority? Do they realize that the people who they're pissing off are actually the very people carrying out the mission?

The higher up in the rank structure you travel, the greater the disconnect from the troops on the ground. It's likely similar in the corporate world, but I'll never know. My next adventure is that of retiring to a tropical island.

Our situation was somewhere in the middle.

Our Warrant was nuts, but our Officer was fantastic. A fearless mother fucker. I was his number two and on several occasions had to reel him in from charging out in front of me.

Captain, what happens if you get blown up?

Our camp itself was simple. It was perfect. There was a tall tower to keep watch from, there were several mod-tents to sleep in and a little kitchen tent stocked with all the Pop Tarts and Nutella we could eat.

Adjacent to our camp was a bombed-out schoolhouse built after the Russians laid siege to this unconquered country. The schoolhouse wasn't ours though. It was home to our Afghan National Army (ANA) counterparts who were always switching their loyalties between us and the Taliban. There was little trust between us, unless they were supplying our drugs.

Giant flower baskets filled with dirt surrounded the camp to act as our walls, while a mile of triple-stacked razor wire was strung to keep out intruders.

It was paradise.

We even had stray cats to keep us company as well as the occasional dog, which would eventually get shot by some trigger happy nobody in our ranks.

I loved our camp. The lifestyle. The rush.

As much as we bitched about it, there's nothing like the feeling of getting shot at or surviving an IED strike. There's nothing like the unspoken bond that manifests between you and your boys when you're over there.

CHAPTER SEVEN

My first day outside the wire involved engaging in a road move. Shit, this was my first day away from KAF, and it was hot. I'd been saturating my body with as much water as I could just to maintain hydration, but this had its consequences. I had to piss, and bad.

I was riding in the gunner position of the turret, with my Sergeant next to me. With nowhere to go, I refilled my empty water bottles that I'd earlier consumed with a new beverage: my diluted urine. Relieved and holding three full bottles of piss, I neatly tucked them above my hatch outside the turret and thought nothing more of them. As would later become routine, we uncovered an IED in the road and stopped to secure the area.

As I scanned the grape fields eager to spot something to shoot at, the sun began to set.

With the sun setting, the horizon became hazy and the

colours began to blur. Before long, my Sergeant began to thirst. Unbeknownst to me, he reached across to my side of the turret and removed one of the piss-filled bottles. This was really his own fault; he never brought his own water in the boat (we called our Light Armoured Vehicles – LAVs – 'boats') and was always grabbing at others peoples water bottles. All the water we drank over there was warm from sitting in the sun, so the tepid temperature wouldn't reveal that something was askew. It was in that hazy period of the evening when colour distinction is difficult at best, so there was no way to distinguish the off-coloured urine from water.

This next part was fantastic.

He removed the lid, took a big gulp, and swallowed. When he recounts the story later, he told me that the 'water' just didn't taste right, so he returned it and grabbed the second bottle. Again he drank, probably bigger this time in order to rinse out his mouth, and fuck, this water tasted off too. My Sergeant was a determined fellow though. In his mind there was no way that three bottles of water could have gone bad, so he removed the third bottle and swallowed hard. Dissatisfied, and unable to rid himself of the putrid taste in his mouth, he commanded my attention and asked me what was wrong with my water.

"My water?" I questioned as I began to look up towards him through the hatch.

Then I saw them.

The three bottles of piss that I'd placed there previously.

Passing me one of the bottles, he said, "Taste this."

Recoiling in disgust, I asked, "You didn't drink those, did you?" and began to laugh uncontrollably.

He sure let me have it. Swatting at me from above, cursing;

all the while I was nearly pissing myself laughing.

It was absolutely priceless.

For the next week or so he wouldn't even talk to me. He'd just look at me and tell me to fuck off.

Naturally, I told everyone.

CHAPTER EIGHT

Most of our early days were spent playing 31 for cigarettes. It's a decent enough card game. As the tour progressed we switched to playing poker for the cash we couldn't spend.

Every time we met up with our buddies from the other platoons we'd swap stories and memory sticks filled with TV series, movies, and porn.

We'd hook each other up with hash or pot.

Every once in a while we'd share a solemn moment.

After one of these encounters, as a friend was leaving, he turned to me and said, "It's too bad. I'm pretty sure I'm going to die out here."

We'll call this a premonition, because he came pretty damn close. While out on patrol, a short time later, he was in the lead position. As he rounded a corner, he stepped right into the sights of a combatant and his subsequent machine gun fire. Like Neo in the Matrix, my friend bridged backwards as bullets ripped through the air where only milliseconds earlier his torso stood erect. This work of acrobatics earned him the esteemed title of 'Mickey the Bullet Dodger.'

CHAPTER NINE

If you've ever read the New Testament, you'll likely recall a story involving these dudes who were unable to get their paralyzed friend in to see Jesus because the house he was in was so crowded. So these resourceful fellows carried their Christopher Reeves-type comrade up to the roof, and then lowered him down through it to land him right in front of the big guy himself.

Before Afghanistan, it had always confused me how you could lower someone through a roof without causing mischief below as a result of falling debris from above.

Afghanistan clarified this Bible story for me.

You see, Afghanistan is living in the year 1390-something, ascribing to the solar calendar or Hamal or some other gibberish. Either way, they're about six hundred and twenty-one years behind our calendar. Look at any of their infrastructure if you need confirmation.

In the province where we were residing, the naturalists were especially simple. They were grape farmers and opium producers. Their houses and compounds were made up of mud walls, their animals lived with them inside these houses, and everybody shit in the streets.

No joke.

They're filthy creatures. The people.

All their hands are shit-stained a reddish-brown colour.

Without modern engineering or design, their flat roofs can't support the weight of the mud tops. Instead of an enclosed roof structure, small ledges are situated at the tops of each of the four walls. Atop these ledges, the Afghanis link branches and hay for protection from the elements.

I didn't know all this on the night of my first mission though, so I was in for a steep learning curve.

Whenever you take position, it's best to perform some reconnaissance to get an idea about the area. Observe the patterns of daily life so that you can notice the absence of normality while out on patrol. Our handover from the previous soldiers was decent. As I noted earlier, however, even if you have all the details of how something functions you'll never really know until you experience it firsthand.

So that's what we did. We armed ourselves to the tits – grenades, ammunition, rocket launchers, and heavy machine guns – and then set off at dusk to perform some recon on the neighbouring pro-Taliban community.

Weighed down excessively by our over-eagerness to become engaged in conflict, it was a slow insertion across the desert landscape and over the wadis. Wadis are either naturally occurring or man-made culverts of water which irrigate the farmland throughout the country. With only one of our guys falling into a wadi during the infill, we arrived at our predetermined grape hut. We planned to scale and then camp out on top of this structure in order to observe the early-morning activities of the people nearby.

A pattern-of-life observation, if you will.

Any time you carry out an activity at night the risk increases. You can't as readily notice the indicators that will uncover either a bomb in your path or an awaiting ambush; we worked at night because the poor bastards we were up against generally weren't equipped with night vision or thermal imagery like we were. We carefully mine-detected the path leading up to the entrance as well as the area surrounding the hut because that's where they chose to plant the majority of their explosives.

After gaining access to the hut, we began hoisting our arsenal up a rickety ladder and onto what I assumed was a solid roof.

You know in high school that god awful-teacher who always reminds you that assuming makes an ass-out-of-u-and-me? Well if he wasn't such a god-awful teacher, I may have reconsidered assuming as I stepped off the ledge and put one foot through the makeshift roof.

Holy shit.

Being far too heavy and inexperienced, I almost met my demise in what would only have been a truly embarrassing tumble through a pathetic excuse of a roof and onto the hard packed ground some fifty feet below.

I have no idea why, but it was at this exact moment that I discovered the mystery behind that New Testament story.

If I learn something new every day, I think I'm doing pretty good.

CHAPTER TEN

Back at camp we were busy setting up our living quarters, erecting tarps over our tent's entrances to act as sun shades. We scavenged wood and stole supplies from the other sections in our platoon in order to build desks and shelves to hold the few belongings that we were able to bring with us.

We strung up rope to hang our clothes from and erected crosses to rest our battle gear on.

We did everything we could do to improve our living situations.

We created spaces to call our own, and then defended them from retributive theft.

We were a bunch of ten year olds with guns. Automatic guns.

We weren't overly fearful of the outcome there, nor did we consider ourselves to be overly threatened, although there were plenty of subtle reminders of the threat at hand.

We crushed our water bottles after we drank them so that the scavenger combatants we were fighting against couldn't use them in their IED construction. This was also why we didn't throw away our used batteries.

We burned all of our refuse.

Up until that point, the only casualties that we had been exposed to were casualties heard of through the voices on the other end of the radio.

The days were long and started to blend together. Weeks disappeared quickly.

Things back home weren't overly enthralling either though. Everybody was just doing the same old shit, carrying on with their boring little lives, not privy to the opportunity of observing firsthand the thread that separates life from non-life.

It took a lot of energy to ensure our safety in the minds of the ones we had left behind, so phone calls home via the satellite telephone decreased in frequency.

The Jack (Master Corporal) in our section kept a detailed account of events during this time, and he wrote a short bio of each of the guys in our section. When I asked him what he wrote about me, he said that I "read and read a lot" and that I also, "speak what's on my mind, uncensored."

Could what I say really be offensive to others?

Fuck it.

I've never been one to agree with the masses.

CHAPTER ELEVEN

Afghanis are weird people.

They wipe their asses with their bare hands and then cook their meals; they pile up three to five people on their 250cc Honda motorcycles and tear off through the desert landscape. The youngest of these vagabonds often hang off the back of the bike for dear life, unaware of the uproar this would cause from an unprecedented number of activist groups which hinder our civilized communities back home.

One of these little guys not more than three years old, approached our camp's front gate and requested medical assistance. The tyke was covered in blood from head to fingertips, an injury resulting from falling off the back of one of the caravan motor bikes.

After searching him and his brother for explosive vests, we admitted them into our camp and our medic began to patch him up. One of the guys in our platoon used to play pro ball before enlisting, and he had a couple of gloves and baseballs that he'd brought with him from back home. He took the liberty of teaching the older brother to play catch and, if only for a moment, allowed that young man to forget about the sick and twisted world to which he was born.

The bloodied tot didn't even cry as the medic removed rocks from his skull and torso. If these kids have one thing going for them, they're tough as nails.

CHAPTER TWELVE

As the days morphed into weeks, combat escalated.

The majority of the fighting occurred in the warmer months of summer when the immigrant fighters could camp outside overnight between engagements. The tension increased as anticipation for something bad to happen mounted.

I remember thinking that I was living in a constant state of stress and wondering if this would be a healthy place to live for the next eight months. It's a game of numbers, right? If you think something often enough, it's bound to happen; excluding the lottery, of course.

It was just a matter of time before we'd get hit.

The antidote for excessive tension is dark humour. In a place where the only surpluses are sand and tension, dark humour is always appropriate.

Have you ever heard that song by Pink Floyd, 'When the Tigers Broke Free'? This became our pre-patrol melody. Sarge and I, along with a couple of our guys, would huddle around the iPod speakers and sing along to the last line:

"Most of them dead, the rest of them dying. And that's how the High Command took my daddy from me."

The other members of our section just stared at us with disgust and disbelief.

We received daily intelligence reports that the combatants in the neighbouring towns had acquired .50 calibre machine guns and sniper rifles. We were told to keep our eyes open for a 'specific make and model' type of vehicle, as it may have been converted into a vehicle-borne IED. The intelligence reports also warned us that local children were being outfitted with explosive vests and to keep them at a distance from our patrols and camp.

None of these reports were ever confirmed, but if the intention was to keep us on high alert, it worked.

My favourite reports were the ones accompanied by actual video footage, a gift from the ever-hovering eyes in the sky, of bombs being dug in or deposits of weapons caches – and then being ordered not to do anything about them except avoid the areas because Higher wanted greater valued targets.

The best reports were the ones that came in three days after we'd been hit by an ambush or stepped on a bomb. Can you begin to empathize with our hard-on for these 'never step outside the wire' soldiers?

Every so often we'd wake up in the middle of the night to the sound of explosions a few hundred metres east or west of our position, and the only thing running through our minds at those times was, "I'd better pretend that I didn't hear that and get some rest; the alarm will sound if it's anything important. Stupid Taliban, didn't they know we're trying to sleep?"

CHAPTER THIRTEEN

One of our most treasured events during our time in Afghanistan was mail drop. Letters and packages from family, lovers, and mistresses were choppered out on pallets and then dropped from the sky into our camp.

During the summer months the National Support Element (NSE, but also known as the No Support Element) allowed our mail and other supplies such as hygiene products and batteries to go undelivered as it was too dangerous to leave the wire in their helicopters.

I don't think that they realized that helicopters fly far above the effective danger radius of most of the weapons known to be operated by our combatants.

It's pathetic, really. An entire organization had contracted the fear. The same fear that motivated our every action has crippling effects on the weaker masses.

Without the pleasure of our correspondence from home,

we took up the psychosis of yelling at flies in our tents. We yelled at them to get stuck on the fly catchers we'd hung. Without the pleasure of our correspondence from home, we took up the psychosis of yelling at the flies that were already stuck on the fly catchers we'd hung.

One day, a buddy and I decided to buy some hash off our ANA counterparts. Employing our translator Ali to speak on our behalf, we approached the highest ranked soldier living in our camp: an ANA Sergeant named Taj. He told us that our request wouldn't be a problem and that he'd come get us in ten minutes or so. Elated, we retired to our tent and yelled at some more flies to pass the time.

When the Ali came to get us, the sun was beginning to set (it seemed like the sun was always beginning to set). We accompanied him to the other side of the camp, and were then directed into the only doored room inside the bombed-out schoolhouse. The room's furniture consisted of a single decrepit mattress lying in the corner. We were instructed to leave our rifles by the door, make our way across the room, and sit on that stained coloured mattress.

Keep in mind that everything this Sergeant says is in Pashtu, which is translated into broken English by our interpreter. Remembering this will add to the ambiance.

Sitting there, stripped of our weapons, we watched in intrigue as Taj removed the tobacco from a cigarette. He heated up the lump of hash in his hand so that he could break it into tiny pieces in his palm. In one fluid movement he hurried the pieces of drug into the cigarette tube and twisted the top.

Stoners all over the world are artists in their own right.

The cigarette was packed, and I remember thinking that

this was a lot of hash to smoke in one sitting. A much larger amount then I was used to hot-knifing back home.

Hot-knifing is where you take a piece of hash and place it on the end of a knife, all while heating the blade so that the smoldering lump of hash can be inhaled.

A few minutes into passing the cigarette tubule around, Taj put out the cig, stood up abruptly, and started spouting off in Pashtu.

Us mattress dwellers both staring up in befuddlement, Ali stood up and walked towards the door.

What the fuck?

Our guns were by the door.

What felt like several minutes later we realized that he stood up to retrieve the pack of cigarettes that lay on the floor near the entrance.

Five Star cigarettes. The brand we were using to smoke the hashish was Pine. "Have you ever smoked hash in a Five Star?" Taj questioned us through the terp (translator).

Half stoned, we replied that we hadn't. Taj proceeded to tell us that, "Hash in a Five Star is the best."

Being the opportunists that we were, we could not decline something better than Pine and both agreed that this proposal sounded good.

Taj, for the second time, began the process of emptying the cigarette of its precious tobacco and removing the hash from the Pine cigarette. All this so that he could fill the acclaimed Five Star tubule.

It was pure artistry.

Before I knew it, the joint was lit and resting between my fingers. I inhaled once, twice, three times…and in a silent challenge uttered by yours truly, I dared a fourth inhalation.

Damn. Who would have known? Hash in a Five Star cigarette was the best.

I picked at something that was edging from the mattress and discovered a pack of matches. Its label read, 'Made in Victory Russia.' Remnants of a war-torn past; a torch that had now been handed to us.

We finished smoking the hash, possibly one toke over the line, and sat momentarily in silence. I was altered; completely euphoric.

Taj began speaking in long sentences. It was always like this. If you were speaking with a local while out on patrol, you'd ask a simple question such as, "Is that your goat?" and the response would evolve over the next two and a half minutes, only to get a one word answer from the translator.

So Taj was speaking and Ali was translating, I was stoned, and all I could think was that this could easily be the scene from some movie.

Before we knew it the sun had completely set behind the panoramic of mountains. We were alone, unarmed, baked, and sitting on a mattress that in all likelihood had been used to sodomize some young boy.

Listen up you pedophiles.

Here in North America you are jailed for your indiscretions, but in beautiful, breathtaking, wonderful   Afghanistan,   not only is child rape acceptable, every elder has himself a prepubescent boyfriend.

I guess it's all relative to where you were brought up.

If I could only count the number of times I've watched some older farmer stick his dick into the young farm help (through the thermals of course, and at a distance of over five hundred metres), well then I'd be able to tell you how many times.

Occasionally, the guys in our platoon would remove their shirts and stroll through the ANA side of the camp just to tease these sexually aroused soldiers with their young, buff, lightly tanned, boyish bodies.

Looking at my partner in crime, we telepathically agreed it was time to leave. Gently interrupting a stoned Taj via our translator, we thanked him and excused ourselves to collect our rifles and begin the star-filled trek back to our side of the camp.

Upon entering our tent, we looked at each other with our bloodshot and glazed over eyes and started to laugh uncontrollably. A trail of hash scent shadowed our every movement.

CHAPTER FOURTEEN

The day we were hit by our first IED, I was wearing my blue bandana under my helmet. If blood would have soaked through it, I'm sure I would have questioned whether I was a 'Blood' or a 'Crypt'. Thankfully this did not happen, and I did not have to contend with this truly difficult dilemma.

Once, while celebrating Canada day back home with friends at a local pub, I decided to dress for the occasion. I wore a red bandana tied to my wrist as well as a t-shirt emblazoned with the Canadian maple leaf. An apathetic attempt at participating in the patriotic festivities.

Another patron visiting the pub was apparently bothered by my chosen attire and confronted me, questioning if I was a 'Blood.' I replied as any self-respecting Caucasian person would, and retorted that 'Bloods' do not exist in white suburbia. He soon retired to his fellow white hip gangster wannabes who were also inside the pub. He resurfaced several minutes later, however this time, flying through the door and landing his fist square against my face. Stumbling backwards, I laughed and gained distance between us by stepping behind a table in order to collect myself.

The little bastard spilt my beer.

To fight or not to fight? There's always a choice.

My laughter emasculated him, subsequently encouraging his second swing. This time, I would not be caught unaware. I gracefully manoeuvred myself away from the trajectory of his fist. This caused his arm to swing past, around, and connect squarely with the brick wall to my right. As his fist exploded with blood, he let out a cry similar to that of my comrade who lay bloody on the Afghanistan desert floor just moments after that first IED blast.

After the blast, I documented that I could still taste the residue and smell of the explosion when I breathed. I made a note to write about it the next day when it would already feel like it had happened weeks before. I went to bed exhausted that night, my ears still ringing – a ringing that haunts me to this day.

The morning of that fateful day, I donned my blue bandana, participated in our Pink Floyd ritual, and then set out for what could only be anticipated as a routine presence patrol. Our target was to link up with some wealthier peasants on the other side of town with the intention of building a relationship with them in order to gather intel.

Who knew that these unsophisticated people were doing the same thing?

One little, two little, three little idiots, all dressed up to die; right?

We filed out of our camp, marching casually through the

village on route to our target location. Upon approaching the white-washed compound walls, a servant met us on the road and informed the residents that we had arrived. Our Sergeant and Ali accepted the invitation for tea and sat down, removed their helmets, and began the fraudulent niceties.

Meanwhile, on the other end of town, a relative of the host planted an eloquently designed DFC (directionally focus charged) IED, along our anticipated route back to camp. This hollowed out artillery shell was filled with homemade explosives similar to those used in the devastating Oklahoma City bombing. Mixed in with the fertilizer were razor blades, nails, and any other sharp objects were used as projectiles. These devices were planted on an angle and regularly ripped through their targets, cutting people in half or opening holes in the sides of our LAV's.

Now that you are more familiar with the details, let's return to the tea party where there's no little rabbit crying, "I'm late. I'm late, for a very important date."

While our leadership and terp enjoyed the sweet succulence of Afghani tea and the debilitating chew laced with opium, the rest of our patrol sat staggered on the path and shot the shit. Early on in the tour many of us claimed that if we were to get injured in battle and sent home, it should happen in the early months so that the money we collected would outweigh the risk we were forced to play. During this sit down, our medic shared our views and commented that if he was going to step on a bomb it had better be today and not two weeks before heading home.

Irony is only funny when it's deadly serious.

Some local children sat down to join us sitting and engaged in our pleasurable game of throwing rocks at each other, another activity we employed to pass the time. This slippery prick of a child dodged one of my tosses and the rock proceeded to hit one of the elders sitting in the tea party, getting him right in the back of his pyjamas (all their garbs resemble cheap pyjamas). I returned his glare with a smile. As the meeting concluded, our leaders donned their fighting gear and rejoined the patrol. As we began to walk away, their servant ran up to our Sergeant and requested help. In hindsight, this was part of their ploy. The elder of the house approached our leader and requested medical assistance for his father who had an infection in his leg. Without thinking – this was our first interaction of this nature – Sarge called our medic forward to examine the invalid. Our Doc quickly dismissed the elderly fellow and rejoined the ranks, reprimanding our Sergeant over our private radios and warning him that situations such as this are common in enemy attacks. The combatants we were up against had learned that if they hit one of our specialized troops (a medic for example) they could cause more damage to our effective strength.

Noted.

We continued on our patrol. This all occurred before nine a.m., so you can rest assured that when the television commercials claim that the army gets more accomplished before nine in the morning, that's not a misrepresentation.

We walked down the path leading from their compound and funnelled into an area that was walled on both sides. As this was not an abnormal occurrence when patrolling the areas of our province, we thought nothing of it. Besides, the walls weren't very tall and one could easily scan the vast expanse of grape fields which covered the area to our right. Farther up the path was a small grape hut accompanied by a shallow culvert which led into the grape field.

It was typical Afghani design.

Unbeknownst to us, this was where they had decided to plant their bomb.

A command string would detonate the device, which was run two hundred metres back through the grape field and on route towards the hostess' location, allowing for an effortless escape for the trigger man. He would disappear back into Afghaniville.

I give credit to these unsophisticated pricks. They're clever.

We were patrolling in the following order: two ANA, then my hash-smoking partner in crime, followed by two engineers who claimed that they had swept the area before we got blown the fuck up. These were the same breed of engineers who, during our workup training, let off a round in the back of their LAV and moments later shot one of their own guys through a range structure. These boys were also of the same breed of engineers who, while residing in our camp, let off a round in their tent and almost shot one of our guys as he was lifting weights in the next bay over. These were the same breed of engineers whom, upon returning to Canada would mistake live ammunition for blank ammunition and shoot another one of their own guys in the leg. Enough said.

Following these engineers was our Sergeant, the ANA Sergeant Taj, our trusted translator Ali, and then yours truly. Behind me were the medic, my fire-team partner, and lastly the Jack who scribed our earlier bios and was subsequently documenting this journey via his digital camera. He caught our blast on video, which can be currently found on the internet under the tag line 'cute goat Afghanistan'. I once showed this video to my therapist during one of our hundred and fifty dollar an hour sessions, and left amused because it looked like she would be the one needing therapy after viewing the clip.

As best as we could recollect, the pyjama wearing prick observed us leaving the Alice in Wonderland engagement, counting off the patrol numbers after the first man passed a particular hole in the wall, until our medic was on top of the anticipated 'x'.

The 'x' marks the spot with a circle and a dot.

Unfortunately, the 'x' is never marked with a circle and a dot.

Since the command line was strung over such a large distance, the subsequent slack may have been the cause for the late detonation of the DFC, causing it to explode just behind our medic.

I was immediately thrown forward, colliding with the mud wall which lined both sides of the path at this location.

Lying face first in the sand beside the wall, I couldn't hear shit. My surroundings were dark; debris fell on the ground all around me.

IED, fuck.

Our training is repetitive and specifically designed to prepare us for such situations. At that moment, these previous exercises came back to me and I recited the required report over the radio, "Contact IED. Contact IED, wait out." Such a report clears the radio waves of all chatter and has the command team waiting for further information from the reporting element. Squinting through the debris-filled air, I saw a body lying limp on the ground behind me.

Shit, I thought, he's dead. I tried to stand but my legs wouldn't move.

Holy fuck, I've lost my legs. I panicked.

Unaware that I had already radioed in a contact report, I called in a second one over the net. I received a response; they were awaiting further details.

My hearing had returned. I looked behind me again, down towards where my legs should have been. I was surprised to find them still there.

I needed to stand up, I thought. I tried, but failed; my body would not support the weight. I tried again.

I could still see that limp body.

I finally made it to my feet and propped myself up against the wall, taking up a fire position, and began scanning the area for antagonists.

"Show yourself mother fuckers – you'll all get shot."

The lifeless body began to moan.

It's then that we realized that our medic had been hit. It's then that we realized that he was still alive.

I wondered about the two men behind him, and called back. They confirmed that they were good to go. Our Sergeant doubled back to the medic's body pulling him by the helmet away from the 'x' and towards my location. Sarge ripped open the medic's combat shirt to expose the wounds, and yelled out for our TCCC (Tactical Combat Casualty Caregiver), our emergency medic, to respond and immediately began treating the wound. A second soldier stepped in to assist him.

The guys in the front and the guys in the rear took up security, scanning the area in the hopes of lighting up anything that moved.

Taj and his ANA soldiers started shooting at the locals as they fled into their compounds. Taking command of the situation, our Sergeant compiled the necessary reports for transmission over the radio and ordered us to get our wounded medic onto the stretcher. The first four guys muckled onto the four supports of the stretcher, and we began our exfil (extraction). We were headed towards an area where a chopper could land safely to medevac our casualty. As quickly as we could shuffle along while carrying our comrade, we navigated our way through the village. Our guns were up the entire time, making it clear to everyone there to stay the fuck out of our way. Every hundred metres or so, we'd switch off carrying the stretcher. Limp bodies are a dead weight, and you tire quickly when moving them.

As we neared the predetermined HLS (Helicopter Landing Site), Doc requested that he walk; we unbuckled him, releasing him from the stretcher. The speed of our exfil increased significantly. We could hear the choppers approaching in the distance.

A nearby LAV met our patrol on the outside of the village and transported our medic the rest of the way. He boarded the bird by walking on his own two feet, and was treated in KAF within an hour of the incident. Well done boys. I guess we passed the first test.

The medics residing in KAF are actual soldiers, not like the other residents I trash-talked earlier.

The HLS was right outside our camp. Having just returned, our Captain had another section of guys spooled up and ready to take control of the location where we had just been hit, but they needed a guide to get them there.

I was selected.

At the end of the day, our officer apologized for sending me back out as he hadn't realized that I had been in the blast also.

Exhausted, shaken, and admittedly scared, I led the fresh

batch of soldiers back to the path that erupted with so much excitement just moments before. The locals had already scavenged the area of most of the evidence we had hoped to collect. The only remnant of the incident was the dark red pool of blood, soaked and half-baked into the path where Doc had been.

While we waited for the bomb specialists to arrive, I rested under a nearby tree as the medics examined me for any injuries. Back at camp, we removed our gear and one of the guys noticed something in the back of my helmet. Removing the cover, we discovered an inch-by-half-inch piece of shrapnel embedded through my helmet's shell.

Damn – that was close. One step less and I'd cease to exist.

Before we had flown out to our camp, those bastards back at KAF briefed us that switching out the painfully gruelling Canadian-made helmet support structure inside of our helmets and replacing it with the American-made padded system would ensure certain death.

Guess they were wrong.

What's funny is that these same people got a hold of a picture of my helmet and, unaware that it employed the American system as they only saw the outside of the equipment, used it to buttress their claim that their helmets saved lives.

One less step and I wouldn't be here to share this tale.

CHAPTER FIFTEEN

Here's another tantalizing tidbit for you. Remember when I mentioned the hope of being plastered over all of the front pages of the newspapers being celebrated as a hero? Well, if I couldn't achieve that, there were certain experiences I wanted to have during my time in Afghanistan in order to return with a well-rounded comprehension of 'war.'

I wanted a gunshot wound.

I wanted to experience a life threatening-explosion.

I wanted to see death.

I wanted to take a life.

Through these experiences, I thought that I could feel war.

I use that word 'war' loosely as I recount this tale; you see, Afghanistan wasn't really a war.

Afghanistan was an occupation.

It was a joke. It was hell.

I'm disgusted by all the veteran status license plates that

have appeared and are sported by all the twenty-something's and KAFites as they drive around our cities. It's even more appalling to see the people driving with veteran status license plates who have never deployed abroad. They obtained this badge of honour through a National Defence loophole. People who have been in the military for three years or more, regardless of experience, can be approved for veteran status plates.

What the fuck?

Veteran? Really? Even calling us Afghanistan combatants 'veterans' is a joke.

If you want to talk veteran, flip through any history book and read about the poor bastards who fought in either of the World Wars, or Korea or Nam.

That shit's fucked up.

I challenge any of you chumps to engage in a real war like those mentioned above. Live through that mess and there's no disputing you calling yourself a veteran. You've earned it.

I know, people got hurt and lost limbs and blah, blah, blah. I feel for them, you, I really do; but you don't play with fire and expect to not get burned. All of the aftermath is calculated risk.

Occupational hazards.

Shit, at least you weren't born retarded. Insert gasp here. Go to hell, you've all been thankful you weren't the poor parents living for those drooling parasites. That would be devastating.

Injuries from combat are anticipated.

CHAPTER SIXTEEN

Its comments like this that allows irony to flourish the way it does. One of the only educated people I know among our ranks always claimed that if he was to get hit, he'd likely lose his eye because he enjoyed reading so much.

Guess what he lost?

After that DFC brought home the reality of our situation, we had no choice but to up our game. At least for a little while, as nothing was happening, but then something happened again.

We'd received intel that there was another bomb in the village where we were hit, and this time we knew its exact location. The informant reported that it was a command-detonated bomb, just like the first one. This could mean many but the most basic design for a command-detonated device is causing a break in the electrical circuit.

For example: You know when you buy a flashlight from the

dollar store and it doesn't work? Well, that's because there's a break in the circuit (unless, of course, the batteries are dead). In most circumstances there's a small plastic coated tab with the words, 'Pull Here'. This tab is wedged between the batteries, effectively breaking the circuit until you pull it free and the flashlight can begin to shine.

Engineering 101: Command line construction. Attach a string to the tab that is wedged between the batteries on the potentially devastating explosive. Run the line a safe distance back, and presto! You have yourself a command line.

Now don't go making homemade bombs yourself.

All of our weaponry was sophisticated and classified; but it really was such a simple art to fuck up someone's day.

There was a bomb. We knew its location, and its type. We wanted the trigger man. Why have just the bombs, when you can apprehend the little prick operating it? We were greedy; doomed to always want more.

A plan was designed, the gist of which was that we'd use two patrolling elements. One would insert under the cover of darkness, propping themselves on a high feature in order to observe the ground below where the command line was run. The second team would depart in the morning, patrolling towards the yet-undiscovered bomb in order to bait the trigger-man out from his hiding place and open up a clear shot for our first element to blow him away.

I was in the baiting patrol group. Lead man.

I'd just been privy to the first blast a few days before, so I was apprehensive of the whole scheme of manoeuvre. The feeling was similar to the one where you're waiting for STD test results while you're looking down at all the red bumps covering your cock.

On the other hand, I was glad I was a part of the bait team – the only way to continue riding is to get back on the horse after you fall off.

The night before the scheduled patrol, I was drifting to sleep reading Tolkien's The Two Towers. I was at the part where the little munchkins were faced with a daunting task and the narrator describes that they were, "like men on the edge of sleep where nightmare lurks, holding it off, though they knew that they could only come to the morning through the shadows."

That's a lie; I wasn't reading it that exact night, although I did read it during our training and figured that if someone has already said it better, use their words.

I trembled as I calculated each step towards the objective. Not overtly, of course, it was a trembling like the time you speak in front of an auditorium for the first time.

I convinced myself that this would be it. The end.

Over the radio we could hear that another call sign was in contact. A gun fight. In the same vicinity an American response team, THOR, had just hit an IED. Only moments later our IRF (Immediate Response Force) struck another.

It was a busy goddamn day.

With the first section dominating the higher ground, we rounded the corner and approached the field which housed the bomb.

This was it. The moment where the thread separating life from non-life becomes visible.

CHAPTER SEVENTEEN

The bomb never went off, the suspected trigger-man having fled the scene. Securing the area, we uncovered a double stacked DFC – two of those crazy ass bombs positioned one on top of the other.

As a result of all the activity that had conspired that day, we were unable to receive support until morning. Rarely, if ever, were the engineers who were patrolling with us, given permission from Higher to disarm the explosives themselves. We were ordered to secure the area and await the support that would arrive the following morning.

We were out for eleven hours that day before another section arrived to relieve our position.

Fresh eyes. We were bagged.

Returning to camp, a message came over the radio from Higher. We were to cease all unnecessary operations due to a lack of resources.

We were only fair-weather soldiers in Afghanistan.

CHAPTER EIGHTEEN

A week after that first blast which claimed a good portion of Doc's arm, I still hadn't received a replacement helmet from KAF. We'd been dropped a flat screen TV, an XBOX 360, a PS3, cheesecake, fucking ice cream; but getting a helmet into a combat zone – now that's ridiculous.

I resorted to borrowing gear from others until my new one arrived. When I finally left Afghanistan at the end of our tour, the nobodies working in the supply stores who issued us our gear tried to make me pay for my damaged helmet because it went missing in transit.

Fucking unreal. They got the old one finger salute in response. The middle finger, in case you were wondering.

CHAPTER NINETEEN

We had four groups (or 'Sections') of soldier in our platoon: Alpha, Bravo, Charlie and Headquarters. Every week we took turns acting as the QRF, or Quick Reaction Force.

Everything in the army is an acronym. Don't trust my interpretation of them either; if I don't know what it stands for, I make it up.

One of our sections, I think it was Bravo, was out on patrol when they radioed back that they had taken contact and were requesting that QRF be dispatched. My section was the QRF that week, so we spooled up our boats and headed out to their location.

One of our boys had been shot. Nothing fatal; a flesh wound in the arm through and through. He was recovered by the medevac choppers and returned home to Canada to begin his multi-year struggle with the military medical system. You'll probably see him on the news complaining about something or other, while attempting to sue the army for forcing him to retire.

Again, shit happens.

Not to sound unsympathetic about any of this, but if you get hurt in the line of duty, take the payout and get on with it. Who wants to be institutionalized by the military for the rest of their lives anyway? Actually, there are plenty of simple-minded folks who do – safe and secure with their paycheck and pensions. Welfare for the middle class. Do this, do that. Everything is laid out for you and scripts are provided to be followed. So yes, what I meant was: who in the free-thinking herd wants to willingly submit themselves to a subservient existence for the rest of their waking lives?

The best thing about this incident was that the kid who was shot appeared to have been shot from behind. Get this too: he was shot with a NATO 5.56 round.

That's what we use.

We suspect that the Loser patrolling behind him was the shooter who let off the round which penetrated his arm. Hopefully in reaction to the enemy contact, but in all reality it could have just been because the guy was about as switched-on as the trigger-happy engineer's folk I mentioned early.

Either way, Shot Guy was safely tucked away at home, and Loser spent a lot of time nursing a sore ankle and skipping out on patrols. We rode him pretty hard about the incident (and anything else we could blame on him).

Fuck it; if there wasn't an enemy to fight, why not take on the next easy target, right?

I'm actually surprised that he didn't end up snapping and slitting all our throats while we were sleeping.

CHAPTER TWENTY

The summer continued like this, bloody as fucking hell. As the temperature increased, so too did our stress levels as well as our cynicism. We collected casualties. People were decapitated. People lost limbs. We were walking through the valley of the shadow of death, pretending to fear nothing, because we wanted to be the baddest mother fuckers in that valley.

Emphasis on wanted to. We were only as tough as our Rules of Engagement permitted us to be. That and our leadership were always being hesitant about making a decision on their own. They were fearful of having to publicly pay for any miscalculations. Few people understand the benefits of never hesitating and always daring.

Sometimes I received a letter or email from home questioning why the villagers allowed the Taliban rule to continue, or asking "Why don't the villagers pick a side?"

Let's step back for a second here and see if we can gain

some perspective. It's very easy to be lulled along and lose sight of the big picture. Stepping back allows us the opportunity to check our focus.

"Why don't the Afghanis pick a side?"

Has it ever occurred to you that maybe they have chosen a side? Maybe they've made up their minds and it turns out that it's not the answer that we had expected or want. Maybe the occupants of this twisted country are sick of our forced occupancy.

Let's see if we can put ourselves in their shoes for a moment; well, in their sandals (nobody wears shoes there). I'll even set the stage with characters you can relate to. You've heard of the Mafia, right? Okay. Well, imagine the Mafia is operating in your city of residence. You go about your business, they go about theirs. No issue. Then one day, you cross paths and find yourself witnessing a crime that the Mafia have just committed. Do you intervene? Fuck no. Only if you had a death wish would you interfere. You turn a blind eye to the incident, they continue to do their thing while you do yours, and a cooperative living arrangement develops.

The cops are pussies and are limited by a surplus of bureaucratic bullshit which ultimately proves their efforts to be ineffective. Should the day arrive that you actually require justice or protection, you'd have to turn to the only force that has the power to provide such a service.

Understand?

Maybe we should stay the fuck out of Middle Eastern conflicts.

I don't think I'm supposed to discuss politics, so let's just categorize this memoir as fiction.

Another thing that pissed me off: our leadership

discrediting the opponents we fought. I'm not a traitor, let's be very clear on that. I just don't have a problem looking at things objectively. I don't think that these combatants are the same combatants of past tours. Honestly, I might even call these guys worthy adversaries. They were tough, deliberate, and intelligent fighters.

Very intelligent fighters.

They were patient. They were meticulous. These guys were determined, always studying how we fought in order to develop their own tactics. After we pulled back following an attack, they would return and assess the battlefield – just like we did. They reflected amongst themselves what worked and what didn't, what to do next time, and what to improve upon. They didn't have the gear that we did, so they fought without body armour. They behaved like ghosts, using their surroundings as their camouflage. Using only basic communications devices, they orchestrated successful ambushes. Knowing that we monitored all of their communications, they employed disinformation campaigns.

Sit there and tell me that they weren't progressing. Tell me that they just keep getting lucky with centre-of-mass shots and successful attacks.

CHAPTER TWENTY-ONE

Every time we left our camp, we were sure to have a contingency plan in place.

"Make sure you take this out of my kit if I eat it (get killed) today."

"You can have this, that, and the other."

"If it's just an injury, wait two weeks before removing any of my things or stealing my bed space. Be sure I'm really not coming back first."

I kept my things neat and organized. Easy clean-up.

It's probably around this time that people no longer wanted to be there. They'd rather have been home with their wives and kids.

CHAPTER TWENTY-TWO

We had fireworks on Canada Day; improvised, of course.

Well, explosions at least.

These jackoffs we fight against repeatedly planted bombs in the same places, almost daily, always along the same path that we didn't have a clear view of. Throughout our tour, we passed up to Higher that we should bulldoze the wall blocking our view so that we could stop wasting time removing the same fucking bombs in the same fucking place.

You know those leaders who are fed great ideas by their employees but shoot them down because they weren't their own ideas? That's our leadership.

Mustard Tiger, Small Arm, and the whole upper echelon.

Here's a quick sketch of Mustard Tiger. He was a man-titted officer who always had a mustard stain on his shirt from using his belly as a table during meals.

One morning we woke up, and guess what? These knuckle

heads had come up with a great idea: they were going to bulldoze the wall. With all their intelligence and combined university degrees, it only took them three months to come up with this plan, and all of it on their own!

It was now mission time. Our job was to go out to the bomb spot, locate the owner of the field, inform him of our plan to tear down his wall, and negotiate retribution.

Upon arrival, we performed a visual VPS (Vulnerable Point Search), before the officer and a few soldiers dismounted for a boots-on-the-ground survey. The hunt resulted in knowledge that the owner of the field lived in a village dubbed KC, a Taliban-supporting town.

We also uncovered a pressure plate and wires and the possibility of a main charge. Mother fuckers. We called in support to destroy the IED, but our Canadian call signs were busy. THOR, our American-counter parts, was in the area and offered to respond to our call. We gladly accepted.

A few days earlier, we had received intel that there was another bomb just up the road from our location at that point. We figured why not get both bombs at the same time? Two birds with one stone, right? Farther up the way, we found two PMN mines mounted atop of two jugs of HME (Home-Made Explosives).

That would have hurt.

THOR rolled in like the cowboys they are, immediately splitting up into two groups in order to dispose of both bombs simultaneously. The thing about detonating explosives though, or any deliberate action in theatre for that matter, is that you have to get permission from Higher.

Higher was not being cooperative, so the Americans said, and we all heard this, "Fuck them, blow it up anyways."

CHAPTER TWENTY-THREE

We got hit from a lot of the same places, regularly enough to say that we got hit from a lot of the same places. One morning through tactical maneuvering, we infiltrated one of these strongholds. We discovered supplies and provisions, IED making components, and uncovered the camouflaged huts they slept in. We burned everything to the ground.

Imagine any of those war movies you've seen where the marauding soldiers pillage villages and burn shit to the ground. That was us – except there were no innocents caught in the mix. Maybe war movies were a poor example, but it really brought on warm fuzzy feelings to watching those shacks go up in flames, reduced to rubble.

KABOOM.

Another contact IED. From a mud hut roof, I watched the explosion detonate and consume most of the Section on the ground below. Oh my God (as irrelevant as he is).

Training had our muscles performing actions without thinking. Before we knew it we were all in fire positions, scanning the area with our ears glued to our headsets.

"All okay," whispered into our ears.

There's no fucking way, I thought. From my vantage point I watched a leg fly out from the blast. "Correction. One KIA (Killed in Action)." We're supposed to say VSA (Vital Signs Absent), but when someone's as dismembered as this guy was, there was no doubt in anyone's mind that he was dead. ANA, Afghan National Army personnel.

Thank Jesus (again, as irrelevant as he may be).

This was a trap. I imagine the guy from Star War's yelling, "It's a trap." But we didn't take notice. We collected ourselves and secured the area. The engineers proceeded ahead to clear a path for us, and soon found the secondary device.

We were in a fucking minefield.

"Nobody move," echoed across our ear pieces. The ANA pers were getting restless, and some of our guys had to forcefully stop them from tromping about.

The dismembered body was removed from its resting place and brought up to us. We were about to send it out to the link up-point beyond, but the engineers insisted on sweeping the way first. Using their metal detectors (or CHIA's) to scan the ground, they got a hit not even five steps behind me. Another IED, but this time it was a wooden pressure plate construct.

What the fuck? I had just led our guys over this exact spot when we entered the area. I had stepped on this piece of shit device. Six of us had stepped on this fucking contraption. It just wasn't our time, I guess.

What made the situation even more disheartening was that all the routes were hard-packed ground. That was usually the only safety we clung to over there. Hard-packed ground, without any loose dirt to give a hint to a planted device, was generally the safe ground to walk on.

We got the body out, which was no small task itself; hauling the weight over mud walls, the whole time blood soaking through the blankets it was wrapped in and dripping onto the dirt beneath us. I remember thinking that this guy was a lot lighter than Doc had been.

I guess half a person would be.

After passing him off, we headed back to the same area to dispose of the shit that we hadn't earlier. The choppers that were now spooled up above us identified two armed men watching us close by. The chopper unloaded two thousand rounds on these guys, and quickly confirmed one of them dead while the other lay bleeding out in a nearby ditch.

Higher ordered us to press forward into the area and conduct BDA (Battle Damage Assessment). Charlie section was closest, so they were assigned with the task. I remember thinking, "Has Higher missed that: a) Charlie is the section that just got blown up; and b) that it's midday, the hottest part of the day; and most importantly c) that we were trapped in the middle of a mother fucking minefield?"

Higher reminded us that it was our duty.

It's easy to play the duty card when you're sitting comfortably in an air-conditioned office, sipping on fresh Tim Horton's coffee while getting your dick sucked by your secretary.

Fuck your duty.

Two more IED's later, Higher made their first intelligent call all day: cancelling the advance. When you're down men and resources, it's a little more than unwise to develop a mission further. It must be nice to sit in air-conditioned offices and watch things unfold from a safe distance.

Don't worry; those pricks will burn in hell.

CHAPTER TWENTY-FOUR

The next morning, we were scheduled to patrol into the same location again. All previous attempts to do so had ended in fire fights and most recently that IED.

Persistence, right? Afghanistan is probably where I learned many of my business skills. Nine out of ten businesses fail; what that tells me is that you have to be willing to start ten businesses before you succeed. You must be willing to fail over and over and over again in order to capture that one golden opportunity.

Embrace the 'f' word. Failure. Not fuck. Even though we walk through the valley right?

Under the cover of darkness, we stepped off for our patrol at zero dark stupid, or 0430h for those not familiar with army speak. We returned back to camp around noon, incident-free, not counting the four IED's we had uncovered.

After spending months going out on patrols lasting eight

hours or more at a time, road trips back home were no longer discouraging. A five hour car ride had become no big deal. Driving to the east coast in one sitting was just like humping all that gear through the desert.

One 's'.

CHAPTER TWENTY-FIVE

Our ever-failing generator and well pump were nuisances that we contended with regularly.

Without the genny running, our lights wouldn't work. Without the lights working, the nights became even longer.

Without the genny running, the well pump wouldn't work. Without the well pump working, we couldn't bathe; bottled water was only for drinking. One of the few luxuries we had to look forward to was a good wash after a hard day's work in the sun, and we became especially intolerable monsters when we couldn't shower.

After one particular stretch of several showerless nights, I formulated a plan. The next time that the power returned, I would fill several jerry-cans with well water and store them behind our tent. This way, when the power failed again, I could hoist the jerry can up onto the wall and open the valve while standing underneath to have a quick rinse at the end of a long hard day. It was genius, and I applauded my ingenuity as I fell asleep, still filthy, yet again.

The next time the power failed and the rest of the guys in my section headed off to bed miserable and filthy, I snuck out back for a quick shower. I re-entered the tent through the back flap, wearing a towel and a giant grin.

I stood there in the entrance until everyone took notice, looks of confusion on their faces.

"One at a time boys," I announced. "We have a private shower out back."

CHAPTER TWENTY-SIX

Every day was an adventure. Before I continue, allow me to address the notion that I've likely shared things with you that I probably shouldn't have. I just want you to know, that I know what I'm doing, and that I'm not going to stop. You wanted to know what it was like. This is it.

I still don't think you could ever really know, but whatever.

Every day was an adventure. This story is probably one of the ones I should exclude.

While out on a road move, we stopped at one of the routine spots where enemy bombs were laid. Me in the turret, the boys on the ground; one of our guys gave me an awkward eye. As I went to press the petzel switch on my radio to ask him what was up, I almost intuitively sensed him telling me not to. My hash buddy. I swear, we had telekinetic powers. He looked around and then pointed towards some upset dirt.

Fuck. An IED.

Every time we went out we found a bomb. Finding a bomb added countless hours to our patrol, and sometimes you just wanted to get back to camp and take your boots off. That day happened to be one of those days.

Carefully, my buddy uncovered the dirt from around the explosive and then assured himself that it wasn't connected to a power supply. He looked up at me once more, and then surveyed the area to ensure that no one else had noticed his discovery. Nonchalantly he picked up the charged artillery shell and tossed it into the water-filled wadi near his foot. Chiming in on the radio, he reported that nothing was found in his area and the officer ordered everyone to mount back up.

That day, we returned to the camp incident free. No harm no foul.

CHAPTER TWENTY-SEVEN

What else do you want to hear?

Ad nauseam. It's time to stop this. All these recollections are bullshit anyways. We made a tour video that documents our haphazard way of life over there, but none of it's real. I gave you antidotes to tantalize your inquiry, but this documentation isn't anything special either. Every combat soldier will tell you a similar story. We've all been through shit; we've all lived this hell. We've all had good days and bad. None of us are special. The problem with our world today, one of our problems, is that everyone thinks they're special. Palahniuk said it best through one of his characters in the novel Fight Club: "Listen up, maggots. You are not special. You are not a beautiful or unique snowflake. You're the same decaying organic matter as everything else."

Earn your fucking self-esteem. Throw away your participant ribbons. Get over yourself.

CHAPTER TWENTY-EIGHT

I'm writing this with the hope that I won't have to tell my story anymore. Not to you. Not to the endless line of nurses and doctors working on my back. Not to the countless therapists passing out PTSD diagnoses like they're free pens at a conference. Not to myself.

I think a lot of the trouble we soldiers have is replaying the memories in our minds. Reliving the experience. Second-guessing – what if? Afghanistan is a haunting shadow.

CHAPTER TWENTY-NINE

I could tell you all the stories about the things we had to deal with over there. The stories about soldiers' parents dying, friends dying; my son dying.

I could tell you about relationships that fell apart. Wives who left. Soldiers who were robbed of all their pay by loveless lovers. All of this while we were 'over there.'

I could. We all could. But fuck it. Not only did we contend with all the violence there – the reality of life's worth – we balanced all that with the daily happenings of life here.

I told you earlier that, "We were on a little vacation from the real world where we would no longer have to worry about paying the bills or keeping up with the Jones'. A little vacation where we would no longer have to deal with the television telling us which pop stars were headed off to rehab. Where the only activities to occupy our agenda would be making sure that our fire-team partners stayed alive so that they could watch our own backs, and then wonder about who our wives would be fucking in our absence."

I told you that, but it's not entirely true. Life didn't go on pause while we were there, we weren't on vacation. We just suppressed all those thoughts to focus on the task at hand: the mission.

We learned to compartmentalize our emotions. We became survival artists. We had to. Higher didn't give a fuck about us. Higher still doesn't give a fuck about us.

Returning home to our units was like returning as a stranger to an unfamiliar land. The next crop of recruits were strutting about with something to prove. The soldiers who had served on the tour before ours carried themselves about in a display of arrogance; as if we hadn't earned our place. Fuck you guys and your winter deployment.

The new leadership set up to command our company were all fresh out of phase training and wherever else they cropped up from, so young that you could still see the vernix on their skin. These were the kids who were going to tell us how to be soldiers? Fuck them and the high horse they road in on. The lieutenant and warrant officer who were fired for their incompetence overseas were now the warrant and officer in charge of our leadership training. Seriously? We had just spent the last two years of our lives away from everything we held close, at cataclysmic costs; and now they wanted to work us just as hard as we had in pre-deployment. And for icing on the cake we got both dipshits who were fired from overseas head the instruction on our leadership courses.

CHAPTER THIRTY

After setting us free in Cyprus for a week, they hurried us through a screening process to determine whether we required professional attention upon our return.

They asked us questions like, "Were you ever exposed to a life threatening incident?"

Seriously.

"Have you ever been shot at?"

"Were you ever in a situation that was morally conflicting?"

"Were any of your friends injured?"

I think the only question on that list that wasn't answered in the positive was the one asking if we had been a victim of sexual assault by a person of authority.

Well aren't we lucky our leadership wasn't clergy?

Everybody in our company could answer yes to the questions associated with combat, and everybody in our company was herded through like nothing was askew.

Ask any of the therapists working with soldiers today, and they'll tell you that the tour that closed of the year in 2010 took the greatest number of psych related casualties.

This isn't a self-loathing, please listen to me, I'm the victim rant. This is a scribbling illustrating the colossal lack of support for your troops.

Fuck your Red Friday.

Fuck your 'Support the Troops' banners and bumper stickers. Support the troops? How about a blow job a day for the rest of our lives?

Remembrance Day is a disgrace. Consider the last ceremony you attended. Twenty minutes of remembrance, and an hour and a half of every thieving business in the community scamming advertising time with the laying of the wreaths.

I had the opportunity to share a few pints with a Medal of Valour recipient – a Medal of Valour that was given for his efforts over there – and I asked him his view on all of this. You see, I want to be wrong. He told me that when people thank him for what he's done, he wants to scream at them, "You're not welcome; fuck you."

You have no idea what it cost us.

We all changed our minds about war while we were over there. We don't give a shit about the people, or you. Period. Maybe we did, once. Now we just want to forget. We want the nightmares to end.

Maybe, if you're a soldier, you'll disagree; maybe your objection is just a façade.

Afghanistan changed us.

CHAPTER THIRTY-ONE

Post Afghanistan, I took an active interest in the brain sciences and learned that we only remember the ideas that we reinforce. All of our memories are reconstructed memories, and their accuracy is not measured in how certain we are or how vividly we remember them. The past is whatever the records and the memories agree upon; we only remember events the way we want them to be.

Most of the day it's easy not to think about one's time there. That is, of course, unless you're still employed by the Department of National Defence. That is, of course, if you're not still surrounded by a hundred other people dealing with similar experiences. It's easy not to think about it if your best friend isn't contemplating suicide, or if your roommate doesn't wake up screaming every night. It's easy to forget when your comrades aren't trash-talking the latest soldier who took his own life. It's easy to forget if you pretend that your fucked-up friend isn't fucked-up. Their lies reflect your own lies, and suddenly you're right back at where you started.

It's also relatively easier during your waking hours. It's those hours in between closing your eyes and waking up in a pool of your own sweat that you have to be weary of. Most of us go on day to day, suppressing our dark passenger. Faking that everything is okay.

You have to fake it before you make it; right?

Most of us just want a refund for the things we've seen. Jack Johnson called them inaudible melodies.

That's it.

Too many stories end with closure. Why? This one doesn't. We may have returned from the battlefield, but the battle is far from over.

Lest we forget.

Let us forget.

AFTERWORD

Well, READER, has it been worth it?

What do you feel?

We started out wondering whether you'd be able to *feel* what it was like over there. So what was your experience? Is there a taste? A physiological reaction? How about an emotion?

This collective experience is the feeling.

All of it. Everything you've felt while reading this text is what a soldier feels in combat.

Anger. Frustration. Disgust. Excitement. Joy. Fear. Love. Hatred. Unease. Trust. Peace.

It's the whole gamut of emotion, and not sequentially or individually either; all at once, all the time.

The language I used was purposeful. The illustrations, equally so. I hope you were able to see that.

You have just invested a piece of your life reading what I wrote and I take this very seriously.

Thank you.

If you've enjoyed it, recommend it. If you'd like to connect, please do.

If there's anything you'd like to say, please feel free to comment online, #NoDiplomacyBook, and leave a review with your favourite retailer.

ABOUT THE AUTHOR

Andrew Lafleche is a Canadian contemporary writer of prose, poetry, and journalism. He was born in Hamilton, Ontario and remained in the Niagara Region before enlisting with the Canadian Forces at the age of 21. Following an honourable discharge from the military in 2014, Andrew published his first book, No Diplomacy, which was inspired by his time serving as an infantry soldier in Afghanistan. He is a contributor to various national and international publications. Andrew now lives nomadically travelling the countryside.